BREAD & WINE

BY DONNA LAGORIO MONTGOMERY

ST. JOHN'S PUBLISHING

6824 OAKLAWN AVENUE, EDINA, MINNESOTA 55435

BREAD & WINE

A St. John's Book/1998

All rights reserved.
Copyright © 1998 by Donna L. Montgomery

Cover art and illustrations by
Laurie Montgomery Walker

*No part of this book may be reproduced or transmitted in any
form or by any means, electronic or mechanical, including
information storage and retrieval systems, without permission
in writing from the publisher, except by a reviewer who may
quote brief passages in a review.*

Published by
St. John's Publishing, Inc.,
6824 Oaklawn Avenue, Edina, Minnesota, 55435.

ISBN 0-938577-17-4

PRINTED AND BOUND IN THE UNITED STATES OF AMERICA
First Edition.
0 9 8 7 6 5 4 3 2 1

DEDICATION

*To
Reverend Joseph Baglio,
my inspiration.*

Contents

Verse	Page
1. Where Is God?	9
2. Prayer	13
3. Miracles	15
4. Touch One Life	19
5. A Drink of Water	23
6. Good Example	27
7. Betrayal	31
8. Retreat	35
9. Loyalty	39
10. Mother of God	43
11. Serenade to Jesus	45
12. Gentle Joseph	49
13. Song of Praise	53
14. Who Is My Neighbor?	55
15. Celebration	57
16. To Give Is to Get	61
17. Love Takes Many Forms	63
18. Building Fund	67
19. Committees	69
20. Lay Person	71
21. Religion Class Teacher	73
22. Community Worship	75
23. Baptism	79
24. Reconciliation	81
25. Communion	83

26. Confirmation 87
27. Ordination 89
28. Marriage 91
29. Anointing of the Sick 93
30. Creation 95
31. Gift of Life 97
32. Lead the Children 99
33. All God's Children 101
34. Testing Place 105
35. Faith 107
36. Hope 109
37. Charity 111
38. Forgiveness 113
39. Compassion 115
40. Serenity 117
41. Holiness 119
42. Gentleness 121
43. Patience 125
44. Justice 129
45. Fortitude 131
46. Long Suffering 133
47. Peacemakers 135
48. Mercy 137
49. Humility 141
50. Those Who Mourn 143
51. Kindness 145
52. Joy 147
53. Who Is God? 149
54. Belief In God 151

55. Our Father 155
56. Our Daily Bread 157
57. Forgive Us Our Trespasses 159
58. Holy Spirit 163
59. Guardian Angel 165
60. Images 167
61. Good Samaritan 169
62. Worship 171
63. Temples of What? 173
64. Living In Peace 175
65. Occasion of Sin 177
66. A Moment to Reflect 179
67. Word of God 181
68. I Live 185
69. Mortality 187
70. Death 189
71. Going Home 191
72. Easter 193
73. All Saints' Day 195
74. All Souls' Day 197
75. A Priest Forever 201

WHERE IS GOD?

Sitting under
a shade tree,
daydreaming
about nothing
of importance
yet everything
that matters,
I watch nature
in all its beauty.

A lonely ant
labors against
overwhelming odds
trying to carry
a burden
over twice its size
to a waiting colony.

Dandelions,
pregnant with seeds,
await their final destiny.
A gentle breeze
is all it takes

to loosen seeds
from moorings,
launching them
away to propagate
their kind.

Robins appear overnight
in Spring,
hopping to the center
of the grass,
giving viewers
a surge of
Spring Fever.

Children play games
with peers,
completely oblivious
to obligations
and demands
that will be
expected of them
at a future date.

In all these things,
God's right at home,
breathing life into
the smallest weed

or managing the
snowfall on a
mountain top.

All these little things
and big ones, too,
are pure God
in creation mode.

PRAYER

We talked with God,
both Father
and Mother,
in a very
formal way
when we were young.
We learned
by rote
standard prayers
that couldn't
vary
by a single word.

Now wisdom
and maturity
have mixed
and tossed
and shuffled
all those pious words
and spit them out
in combinations
sounding more like
conversation.

I speak to
God the Father
and Mother
as a mother myself,
who has had to deal
with errant family,
thus learning both
compassion and forgiveness.

Mother God
understands my
shortfalls,
while Father God
nestles me in
strong, protecting arms,
and tells me
I am trying
and that's
what's important.

And God blesses me,
and sends me out
again
with knowledge
that I'm loved
and will never be
alone.

MIRACLES

Since Christianity began,
people have
looked for miracles
and apparitions
unexplainable
in human terms.

Holy people
argue about
authenticity,
while ordinary people
readily believe
anything unusual
or other-worldly.

How blind we are
to so many miracles
we see, hear,
and experience
everyday.

A newborn's cry,
a loving act,
eyes and ears
that see and hear.
We can think a thought
or feel the hurt,
yet never understand
daily miracles for
what they are.

People helping people,
man walking
on the moon,
harnessing nature's power,
and having power
for us to harness.
Lakes, rivers,
and oceans plenty,
furnish food and drink
for us to grow.

A family's bond
that doesn't sever,
getting up
when we're down,
even in our most trying
and desperate times,
sacrifice endured
for love,
excitement felt
when holding
our lover's hand.

Each moment
is a miracle
simply by the fact
that it is.

TOUCH ONE LIFE

Sometimes
the magnitude
of our world
overwhelms me.

Standing next to
a mountain,
flying above
the earth
in a plane,
sailing on a ship
at sea,
these things
shrink and
humble me.

Stars, wind,
sun, rain,
are not interested
in my single life.
They will continue
their methodical

patterns and cycles
with or without
my presence.

If I can neither
cause the sun
to forget to rise,
nor stars to
drop out of the sky,
while wind and rain
pursue their own
agenda
and neighbors
one block away
don't even
know my name,
then I must
set my own agenda
and start by
touching just one life.

Starting with myself,
I'll get to know me better,
then my neighbor

as myself,
and then my
neighbor's neighbor.
Hopefully,
the ring of love
will touch first one life,
then one after another.

A DRINK OF WATER

"I thirst,"
He said
when dying
on the cross.
They thirst . . .
the babies
at their
mothers' breasts.

Toddlers trust
caregivers
will help them
quench the thirst
they recognize
but cannot
sate themselves
without help.

The old and infirm,
sick and dying,
must often rely
on others' charity
to satisfy their thirst.

A drink of water
given with love,
is the opportunity
so many have
to help
a gentle soul
in great discomfort,
thereby helping
themselves
the most.

"I thirst."
A drink is asked for
by the dying Christ
upon the cross.
No one came to
give Him water.
Vinegar was all
He got.

May we always be
open to each other's
basic needs
and recognize the
primal thirst
seen daily

in our neighbor.
If we give water
to the least of us,
it's given to
the dying Christ.
A drink of water;
a glimpse of Eternal Life.
No one need
ever say,
"I thirst."

GOOD EXAMPLE

A mother
bends to reach
her child,
then points to
one of nature's
wonders
and shares
her knowledge.

Teachers
share information
with students
on a daily basis,
sometimes over
and over
with consistent
patience.

Chronically ill
plan when able
to ease their passing
for survivors.
Personal treasures
are divided,
and funeral services
are often planned
by them
to ease death's burden
for surviving
loved ones.

Children
watch parents
go about
their daily chores
with good cheer
and love
in their hearts,
then wordlessly
and unknowingly
follow their example.

Executives in business
who lead by
good example,
make workplaces
pleasant and enjoyable,
creating jobs
that stimulate
and challenge workers
to do their best.

Good example:
costs nothing,
can't be bought,
stimulates the best in us,
and makes givers
and receivers
happy.

So what are we
waiting for?

BETRAYAL

They sat
around the table
partaking,
yet not really
understanding.
It was the last
meal of celebration
the little group
would ever have.

He offered them
bread,
and told them
it was His body.
He offered them
wine,
and told them
it was His blood.

Amid the fellowship,
and before
the consecration,

Jesus dropped
a bombshell.
Before the night
was over,
He said,
He would be
betrayed
by a kiss.

The twelve apostles
were shocked,
but incredibly
each asked this man
if it was he
who would be the
betrayer.
Didn't they know?
Weren't any of them
confident enough
to trust themselves?

"Is it I, Lord?"
How many times
He heard
the timid question.
"Is it I, Lord?"
At last He looked

with heavy heart
into one man's
questioning eyes
and acknowledged,
"Thou hast said it."
And Judas
left the room
and did the deed.

RETREAT

Retreating
into hidden places
in our minds,
we begin
rediscovering things learned
but soon forgotten:
memories both sad
and happy,
and others we
misplaced so long ago.
In solitude
we unlock
forgotten chambers,
releasing from our minds
so many yesterdays.

Quietly we begin
rediscovering ourselves,
and also our Creator
who waits patiently
for us to acknowledge
our dependence.

Reality checks
bring to mind
busy daily routines
that snatch us
from quiet moments
when we could
be silently renewing
our friendship
with God.
Instead, we
fill our days
with what we call
necessities,
but they really aren't.

Wasting time
fits nicely into
daily routines,
fooling us about
what we accomplish
each day,
while over-programming
our simple beings

into believing
hours worked
imply importance.

Retreat;
Reflection;
Humility;
Holiness.

LOYALTY

Jesus did
His first miracle
because
His mother asked.

When He traveled,
women saw
that He and His apostles
were fed
and housed.

Tears of a sinner
bathed His feet
and her hair
dried them.
He praised her
to His men.

He raised
a woman's brother
from the dead
because of her faith.

When Jesus
carried the cross
to His death,
a brave woman
mopped His brow
and was blessed
with His image
on her cloth.

Women remained
by His feet
while He hung
on a cross of wood,
nails piercing
hands and feet,
a ghastly sight,
and yet they
didn't faint
or leave,
but stayed
until the end.

Women prepared Him
for burial,
came to guard Him,
and were the first
to discover Him
risen.

Women told the men,
but the men doubted
the resurrection.

How Jesus
loved the women.
How He honored them.
His mother Mary
never needed burial.
She rose to
join her Son.

Blessed are all
the loyal women.
How He loved them.

MOTHER OF GOD

Gentle Mary,
what an awesome turn
your life took
when you entered
your teens.

At the age
you became a mother,
girls today
are just outgrowing
Barbie dolls
and starting
junior high.
Imagine that!

Were the beginning
teen years then
so different from
those same years now?

Were you restless
to get on with
your life,
or content to be
a young teen
expecting a baby?

Humble, obedient Mary.
You met God's challenge
lovingly
and with poise.

How mature
you must have been
to understand
God's words
and fulfill them.
You were
little more than
a babe yourself.

Help me
to be more like you,
trusting God's word
to surround me
with loving arms
and guide me
to my destiny.

SERENADE TO JESUS

My dear little child,
I've waited for you.
Even though I'm young
and was unprepared
when you were conceived,
the anticipation
of your coming
set my heart singing
and my feet dancing.

How could
God our Father
choose me
to be your mother,

when I'm so young
and come from such
a humble background?
You're so precious
a person
to be placed
in my care.
What was God
trying to tell the world?
Why did we
have to take the manger
away from animals
so you could
have a crib
in which to rest?

The ways of the Lord
are strange indeed.
I've had visions
of the sadness
the future holds
for you, Joseph, and myself.
I shudder
when I see
those things
in my mind's eye.

My dear little child,
all I can do for you now
is love you
with my whole heart,
teach you
what I know,
play with you,
guide you,
and be there for you
unconditionally.

We will live for
the moment,
treasuring and hoarding
whatever time
we'll have together.
Much of your time
on earth
will be as a
child and adolescent.
I will enjoy those years
with you.
When your public life begins,
I will support your choices.
My dear little child,
we will always
face life together,
praising God.

GENTLE JOSEPH

Gentle Joseph,
foster father to our
brother Jesus,
what were your
thoughts about
such a noble job?

Was Jesus ever naughty,
or was that
impossible?
Did He apprentice
to you
in carpentry work?
What kind of
teenager was He?

The Bible
doesn't tell us
much about you.
I picture you
holding your baby
with calloused hands

in muscled
carpenter's arms.
How safe Jesus
must have felt.

Did you make
a little table and chair
for Jesus
to sit at
and play?
I'm sure you made
wonderful, creative
wooden toys for Him.
Did He follow you
around the shop
and play on
sawdust-covered
floors?

I'll bet
yours was a
quiet family
that enjoyed
each other's company.
Did you teach
your Son to pray?
Did you talk to Him

of life?
Tell me what
you talked about,
then teach me
how to pray.

SONG OF PRAISE

Joyful voices sing
in praise of
God the spirit
of new beginnings
and immortal endings.

Everywhere one looks
God is witnessed.
We see new life
appearing in nature
each spring,
in the welcoming
shade of trees
on hot and humid
summer days,
in the kaleidoscope
of fall colors,
and then in winter's
harsh reality
of blinding snow
and dangerous ice.

Praise God
for beauty
which differs
in the eye
of each beholder.

Praise God
in every way:
cardinals' songs,
comets' tails,
red tomatoes,
children's laughter,
tender touches,
sharing lunches,
lovers' silence,
mothers' hunches.

Praise God
for morning breaking,
and at day's end,
for sun setting.
And praise God
I'm here,
a human soul,
to witness life
and be a player.

WHO IS MY NEIGHBOR?

"Love thy neighbor
as thyself."
Nothing is too good
for myself!
I buy perfumes
for my body,
eat too much food,
want too many clothes
and other things.
I worry about
my comfort
and other equally
worldly objects,
denying myself little.

But I must love
my neighbor as myself,
starting with next door,
then community,
city and state -
even those
I really don't
care for.

Those who suffer silently
in countries
ruled by terror,
intimidation and hatred,
are my neighbors.
People who are
a rainbow of colors,
languages and traditions
with mutual needs,
loves, and desires,
are my neighbors.
Harmony is our goal
when we recall
who Jesus befriended.

Who is my neighbor?
Everyone who
needs a friend,
and even those
who don't.

CELEBRATION

I come home
from the funeral
of an old friend,
a woman
too young
to die.

We were told
this was a
celebration

of our friend's
passing to her
eternal home.

We were told
to rejoice
in this happy time
of passing
from one life to the next.

But I can't celebrate!
I need to grieve,
be angry,
hate death,
weep,
be numb!

My friend
was too young.
She needed more time
to smell the roses
and walk the earth.

She needed time
to have grandchildren
and a chance to know them.

She was entitled
to a few years of peace
after raising her children.

A new career
was starting for her
mid-life,
with brand new
college diploma in hand,
beginning a teaching career.

Death cheated her.

When I become
immortal
it will be easy
to celebrate new life.
But for now,
my sadness weighs
too heavy:
I cannot celebrate.

TO GIVE IS TO GET

We give our hearts
and get abundance;
we give to the poor
and enrich our spirits;
we give to children,
and love fills our being.

When people give
of themselves
or possessions,
expecting nothing
in return,
they receive
the most.

Giving time,
without thought
of what will be missed
when robbing hours
from busy days,
usually misses
nothing
that can't be done
another time.

Giving is the purest form
of receiving.
A single apple seed
given to the earth,
rewards us with
a tree that flowers
in the spring
to feed our souls,
and grows fruit
in summer
to feed not only
our bodies,
but those of
many other
people and animals.

And so it is with us.
When we sow seeds of
love, kindness, and generosity,
we reap daily blessings
reflecting much more
than we give.

LOVE TAKES MANY FORMS

A baby
looks at mother
with unselfconscious
adoration.
Young students
love a gentle
but firm teacher.
Grandparents marvel
at the wonder
of a new generation.

Love is in
a mother's eyes,
a lover's kiss,
a friend's touch.

Love is a presence
that lights up a room
when someone special
enters.

Love isn't
color conscious,
nor does it see
human flaws
so evident
to those whose eyes
are blinded
by prejudice
and an absence of love.

Love patiently
waits out human storms
and staunchly
remains a friend
when others leave
for companions
easier to love.

Love doesn't
come and go
like leaves on trees
or frost on windows.

Love is pure,
love is unselfish,
love is giving,
love is gentle.

We don't know
how it starts
or when it dies.
Love is simple
in its magnitude
and complex
in its simplicity.
We have to
work at love,
because it's
not always forever.

BUILDING FUND

"The Building Fund."
These dreaded words
pit normally well-balanced
church members
and neighbors
against each other
in the name of religion.

They fight about need,
affordability, and cost,
then size, shape,
and what to build.
The latest
architectural bonanza
seems to be
The Gathering Place;
before that came
The New Church.

"The Building Fund:"
possibly
the greatest divider

in a community.
Change can be painful,
but unnecessary change
can divide.
Members need to
review the need,
consider all options,
and abide by
majority decision.

"The Building Fund:"
a challenge to
humility, courage,
intelligent decision making,
and prayer.

COMMITTEES

Parish Council
Administration
Finance
Religious Education
Adult Education
Social Justice
Deacons
Marriage Counseling
Baptism Preparation
Engagement
Funeral
Music
Liturgy
Social
Trustees
Etc.

You name it.
The church has it.
God help us.

LAY PERSON

Come walk with me
on my journey
to heaven.
I don't know
the intricacies of faith
as the religious do,
but in my heart
I know what's right,
and what's wrong.

I know when
people say,
"You deserve
this good luck,"
that it's not true.
I deserve nothing,
because if I deserve,
so does everyone else.
All people, whether
suffering injustice, pain,
hunger, or untimely death,
also deserve good luck.

I know
children are innocent
at birth,
but as they
develop and grow,
they're too often
scandalized by adults
they rely on
for direction and example.

I know
when I'm able to
ease another's pain,
love a child,
feed the hungry,
clothe the naked,
visit the sick,
and love my enemy
who is my neighbor,
I have risen
to my calling.

RELIGION CLASS TEACHER

Put on your
crash helmet,
roll up your sleeves,
and enter the world
of religious education.

Are you ready
to invest credits
in heaven's bank?
Are you a
stalwart soul
ready to
try and interest
children,
after their long
school day,
in the words,
teachings and philosophy
of Jesus?

Are you willing
to suffer martyrdom
at the hands
of children?

If so,
religious education teacher
is the job for you.

But along with
the downside
comes a strong knowledge
that lessons taught
have not fallen completely
on deaf ears.
Teaching and dedication
of religion teachers
isn't wasted on
the young.

As sure as the sun
rises in the east,
and sets in the west,
the tiny slivers
of religion
poked under
a child's skin
will resurface
in later years
to prick the conscience
with truth.

COMMUNITY WORSHIP

How comfortable
to worship God
within my own mind,
in my own way.
No listening
to others
pontificate
on their own
soap boxes,
just simply
independent worship.

But Jesus said,
"Wherever two or more
are gathered
in my name,
I am in their midst."
Why must He always
shake up
my comfortable
little corner
in the world?

Must I always
have to sit
among the masses
of people
with crying babies
and bad colds,
in overcrowded churches,
listening to less than
theatrical excellence
in service and sermon?

Yes, I must,
because it's in
the community
we find church.
Community is church.
Christ told His
well-meaning apostles,
trying to hold back
children at His
community services,

to bring them
to Him for
"such is the
kingdom of heaven."
A glimpse
of future life
seems to tell us
that heaven is community.

BAPTISM

Jesus entered the Jordan,
walked up to
John the Baptist,
and asked to be baptized.
Although Baptism
was unnecessary
for Him,
Jesus chose to
teach by example.

Churches baptize
for different reasons:
to cleanse, initiate,
or name new members.
We're told it's one of the
outward signs of faith,
instituted by God,
to give grace.

By celebrating baptism
publicly, and in the
presence of friends,
we acknowledge

the importance
of God in our lives,
and the real
and symbolic need
for sacraments.

Baptism is our
birth again,
this time into
spiritual life.

RECONCILIATION

Mea culpa,
mea culpa,
mea maxima culpa.
They come in numbers
large and small;
sinners young
and sinners old,
in God's name
asking forgiveness.

    Christ is gone,
    but in His place
    sits an ordained
    man of the cloth.
    He listens
    with attention
    to each mind's own
    frank confession.
    He was told
    to meter punishment
    with wisdom
    and compassion,

and support
each sinner's goodness
which outshines
a moment's weakness.

God forgives
and loves us still,
it's no secret,
we've been told.
But it has to be
depressing
for the Spirit
to hear confessed
the same sins
repeated daily
with much remorse
but less resolve.

Forgive us Father,
we your children
who have nailed
your hands and feet
to the filthy
wooden cross
of Calvary
because it's
uncomfortable
to change our ways.

COMMUNION

Communion:
a piece of bread,
a cup of wine,
a meal shared
in community,
and believed to be
either representative of,
or the body of,
Christ.

If we doubt
Jesus' divinity,
we need only listen
and understand

what simple acts
He did
two thousand years ago,
that have been
passed down
generation after generation.
An ordinary man
living Jesus' life,
would have
soon been forgotten.

Evidently, Jesus' quiet,
non-violent behavior
didn't belong to
an ordinary person.
He raised the dead,
forgave sinners,
and loved His enemies.

When soldiers came
to get Him
for crucifixion,
nourished with
the bread of life,
He went peacefully.

This humble
God-man,
took bread
in His hands and said,
"This is my body,
take and eat."
After they ate,
He took a cup of wine
in His hands,
blessed it, and said,
"This is my blood
which will be shed
for many
for the forgiveness of sins.
Do this
in remembrance of me."

Two thousand years later,
we still do.

CONFIRMATION

Let the battle begin!
We put away
toys of childhood
and focus on
responsibilities
of adulthood.

Self-centered
priorities of youth
supposedly give way
to outreaching
actions of age.

We are
soldiers of God
inspired by the
warrior Spirit
in each of us
to find God within
and share that
Light
with family,
friends, and neighbors.

Confirmation:
the formal passing
into spiritual adulthood,
acknowledging need
for recognition
of each person's
God-given talents,
and the necessity
to share them.

Personal actions must better
our neighbor's condition,
not hamper it.
This is
our mandate.
These are
God's orders.

ORDINATION

Christ called
fishermen to leave
family and follow Him.
What did Peter
tell his wife,
and was she agreeable?
A tax collector
was called,
various others,
but mostly
humble fishermen.
Twelve were chosen
to be His apostles,
then others as disciples.

Instructions to
His men
were simple:
make ready
their accommodations.
Apostles were
advance men
preparing Jesus' way,

and crowd controllers
when He spoke.

The men were told
to enter a town
and seek food
and shelter
for the group.
If the town
refused them,
they were to
shake off the dust
of the place
and move on.

Apostles and disciples
were scorned
and failed,
yet pressed on.
They were servants
of both the people
and Jesus,
who in turn
served them
... family men
and bachelors,
these first
bishops of the church.

MARRIAGE

God bless
this new beginning
as man and woman
become husband
and wife
in God's eyes
and those of
the state.

May this fresh
new love
renew itself daily
and be strengthened
in hard times
even more than
in the good ones.

May children
be welcomed
at all times
and stabilize
the marriage
with selflessness
and generosity.

May each couple
walk in harmony
and equality
for many happy years,
thinking first
of each other
while reaching out
instead of in.

And may their
shared road to heaven
be paved with
good deeds
rather than
forgotten promises.

We're all travelers
on the same
journey,
trying to reach
the same
goal.
Together we make
the trip a struggle
or a pleasurable journey.

It's in the attitude.

ANOINTING OF THE SICK

The anointing
of the sick –
previously,
only those people
who were dying
received
this blessing.
Now, the ill
find strength
in the holy oils,
and protection
from death
of the soul
if not the body.

Approaching the time
of final goodbyes
as life wears on
to its end,
people review
the ups and downs

of either
a long, full life,
or one so short
it hardly
had time
to begin.

We think of
Mary Magdalen
as she washed
the feet
of Christ
with her tears,
and anointed them
with precious oils.
This was a predictor
of Christ's death,
and first step
to His resurrection.

God became man;
God died;
God rose,
never to suffer
again.

So will we all.

CREATION

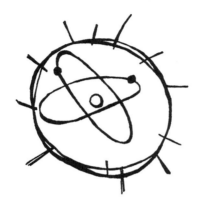

Nothing.
Atom.
Division.
New life.
This is creation.

(But where did
the atom
come from?)

GIFT OF LIFE

I gift you,
my child,
with the basic gift:
Life.

Working in partnership
with our Creator,
I am the vessel
that allows you
to grow
after the
hand of God
creates you.

For almost
everything else
in my life,
I will be trained
and guided,
instructed and tutored.
But the most
awesome,
magnificent,

overwhelming job,
that of parent,
is taken so lightly,
few take classes
in preparation
before
becoming one.

The gift of life
is the alpha
and omega.
Without it,
nothing else matters,
in fact,
without it . . .
nothing.

LEAD THE CHILDREN

Pipe the tune
with merry heart;
children skipping
in crooked lines,
following blindly,
completely trusting,
so don't take advantage
of innocent hearts.

Only tomorrows
lie ahead,
yesterday's forgotten
before it leaves.
The present just counts
and instant gratification;
first food for the body,
then hugs for the soul.

Innocent newborns,
trusting toddlers,
youngsters and teens
all needing love.
Hearts filled with song
and happy abandon,
carefree days
with refreshing
night's sleep.

This is what youth
is supposed
to be like;
but unfortunately,
it's not always so.
"Woe to those
who scandalize children."
God's words
are fair warning
to all.
We can't always
be perfect,
we're human,
God knows.
But be warned,
be an example,
and be loving
to young souls.

ALL GOD'S CHILDREN

We come
from countries
large and small,
north, east,
south and west.
We come with
coats of fur,
robes of gold,
clothes patched
until cloth
is hard to find,

the naked,
rich and poor,
speaking languages
as varied as
our colors.

We come
from farthest corners
of the globe,
desolate land
or prolific rain forests.
Our single
similarity
is diversity.
No two of us
are alike,
with different
needs and wants.

In our families
we find
mutual interests
to unite
and bond us
while enjoying
the relaxed environment
familiarity promotes.

We take care
of each other
and rejoice
with family
when good things
happen
to good people.

We need
to take this
one step further.
Being children of God
makes us all
brothers and sisters.
Knowing this,
how can we
hurt one another
by word or deed?

TESTING PLACE

Life begins
with complete
helplessness
so people
may rise
to the occasion
as caregivers.
All are given
free will
to make their own
choices.

During early
family years,
parents have
many opportunities
to put aside
their own desires
and fulfill those
of their children.

At work,
employees

and employers
all have
numerous chances
to help their neighbor,
share the work,
recognize
a job well done,
or share counsel
over a cup of coffee.

And when life
nears its end
and eternity
lurks around
the corner,
a final test comes
with the humility
to let oneself
be helped,
if necessary.
How well we test
in this world
may determine
our degree of joy
in the next.

FAITH

I do not see
a physical God,
but I believe.
Proof is visible
whenever my eyes
are open,
and also at rest
when body functions
      slow down
      to rejuvenate
      God's creation.

I believe
the blueprint of a body
had a mastermind
of immortal dimension.

I believe in
interaction of earth,
sea and sky,
the magnificence
of nature, our minds,
the food chain.

I believe humans
work in partnership
with God
in the creation
of new life.

I believe in
the sacredness of life,
that death is a part
of every life,
and that God decides
when life begins,
and when it ends.

I believe
we were known
at the beginning
and will be
at the end.

I believe in
life in the womb,
life on earth,
and life after death.

I have not seen,
but I believe.
And that is
my faith.

HOPE

Optimism falters
because we're human,
and rekindles
for the same reason.

Failure is part
of every life
and is often
the flame that
fires steel.

Why do we
continually get up
after falling,
and keep trying
until we come
as close to success
as we're able?

Hope.
Hope helps us
try our best
to succeed

where we have
previously failed.
It shows us
what can be
if we continue
against all odds,
winning some battles
while losing others.

Hope buries pessimism
with all its
negative vibrations,
giving us incentive,
as well as the drive,
to surmount negative odds.

Hope nurtures faith
and compliments charity.

CHARITY

Love and charity
are quite different
by definition,
but similar
in more ways
than not.

Love represents feelings,
while charity speaks
to alms.
But giving
at its richest
is based on
love of people.

By the pure
accident of birth
and blend of genes,
our die is cast.
Family and environment
take the reins
after genes decide
who runs the race.

Those receiving charity
gift those to whom
they give the opportunity
to share,
Christ being
the living role model
of gifted
and giver.

Christ's death on the cross
showed His love
for all people
and made everyone
the recipients
of His charity.

FORGIVENESS

God the Son:

was ridiculed
... and forgave.
was humiliated
... and forgave.
was tortured
... and forgave.
was killed
... and forgave.

Can we do less?

COMPASSION

Your shoes
belong to me
and mine
to you.
I must
take your suffering
and wear it
as my own.
And if
my suffering
lessens yours,
you gain
a brief respite
on your difficult journey
in this life.

I will
wear your concerns
and try to
minimize them
so you can cope
when I am absent.

I cry for
you and yours
and wonder why
some lives are
so much easier
than others.

God loves
all of us
the same
and demonstrated
his compassion
time after time.

By the accident of birth,
we each live
different lives.
Those in need
of compassion
are blessed by God.
Those not in need
of compassion
have the opportunity
to be blessed
by sharing what
they were gifted.

SERENITY

Serenity comes
when we put away
things of this world
and focus on
the next.
There is a peacefulness,
a tranquility,
in letting go.
If neither the
birds of the sky,
nor lilies of the field
need to worry,

why should we?
If God knows
their needs and desires,
and they can't
tell Him,
how much more
is He aware of
our needs
because we can
put voice to them.

We need little,
lest worldly possessions
get in the way
of our serenity.

HOLINESS

Holiness isn't owned
by publicly demonstrating
outward signs of it
to impress friends,
neighbors, and family.

Holiness isn't about
hair shirts,
worn shoes,
or holes in knees.
It doesn't become
owned by someone
because they
put on
a priest's collar,
or a nun's habit.
It knows few
TV evangelists
with million dollar
needs and budgets.

What holiness is
becomes elusive,
at best,

when we try
to put a finger on it.

Holiness is in
the bravery
faced by those
with handicaps,
fatal illness,
or terrible loss.
It's owned by
people who support
children as well as
the old and infirm.
It belongs to those
who praise God,
love their neighbor
as themselves,
and comfort
the ill and dying
while seeing God
in all creation.

Holiness is a gift
we must earn
and into which
we slowly grow;
but once we own it,
it's hard to lose.

GENTLENESS

Rain falls gently
in spring,
nourishing new growth.
Summer sun
invites flowers
to bloom
and grass to grow.
Fall leaves
turn color
at showtime

and gently fall
to earth
so trees can
hibernate.
And winter's snow
can be
gentle and soft
as well as a
biting blizzard.

The gentle part
of nature
reminds us
of God the Son
who walked
the roads,
becoming a
public figure
for only three years.

His journey
was gentle
in His passage
and presence,
turning the
other cheek
while patiently
teaching people.

His message
was new,
revolutionary,
yet He practiced
tolerance
in many ways.

And when
those He helped
became
the maddened crowd
that tortured
and then killed Him,
the picture
in our mind's eye
is of a silent man,
gentle until the end.

PATIENCE

"Please, Lord,
give me patience,
but make it
fast."

How often
we feel this way,
recognizing the need
for patience
but the lack
of time
to wait for it.
Yet so many
beautiful things
require this virtue.
We cannot
rush a rose,
the first robin
of spring,
ice thawing
on lakes,
children's youth,
or an elder's speed.

Friendships
deepen with longevity,
marriages are enriched,
and fruit ripens
with patience.
The metamorphosis
of caterpillar
to butterfly,
tadpole to frog,
helpless newborn
to walker
in one year,
take their own time
and patient waiting.

We are told
about God
when we're young,
sometimes lose track
in middle years,
then usually
find God again
in later years.

And God
walks silently,
consistently,
and patiently
with us
on our journey
... whether we want
company
or not.

JUSTICE

Those who fight for justice
find the battle difficult,
thankless, and lonely.
Anger is hard to handle
when looking at the obvious
and realizing how injustice
is so easily tolerated,
because, simply,
to fight for justice
might interfere with someone's
isolationism, privacy,
or leisure time.

Apathy is at the front
of our thoughts,
urging us to
ignore injustice
because the matter
doesn't involve us personally,
or it invades
our private space.

The unjust trample over
the weak and helpless,

young and old,
poor and reliant,
getting ever bolder
with each victory,
challenging the comfortable
to confront evil
and preserve,
protect, and defend
the rights of others.

We need
courageous role models
to lead us
to a higher ground,
setting the example
for us to follow.
It may cost dearly
of our time,
and even our money,
but the benefit
to our self-esteem
tells us we have
no other choice;
justice is the right
of everyone.

FORTITUDE

At some time
in all lives
people have
the opportunity
to practice
courage under
affliction or privation.
How we measure up
in difficult situations
makes us
more understanding
in our dealings
with others.

So many
buckle under
to pressure
from peers,
taking the easiest,
less courageous way.
Everyone appreciates
comfort
and freedom
from pain,
but if it
must come,
the gift of fortitude
is ours for the asking
to help us
on our journey.

LONG SUFFERING

Heaven
means different things
to many people,
but to the
long suffering
it must be
the ultimate joy:
freedom of mind
and body
from suffering.

Physically
or spiritually ill,
mentally distressed
or abused,

and countless souls
who experience
injustice and prejudice,
will suffer no more.
God will
ease their burden,
rewarding them
with comparable joy
and freedom
from all pain.

If we mourn,
we will be comforted;
if we hunger
and thirst
for justice,
we will have it.
The merciful
shall have mercy,
and the persecuted
will have
the kingdom of Heaven.

This is the promise.

PEACEMAKERS

Blessed are the
peacemakers:
they will be
recognized
as the
children of God.

It becomes difficult
in this
litigious world
to search for
and find
peacemakers:
the person who will
turn the other cheek,
forgetting self,
to bring peace.

We mustn't
confuse
justice
and peace,
or substitute

peace
for justice.
If an injustice
has been done,
peace will come
after justice
has been served.
There is peace
in justice.

The two
cannot be separated.

MERCY

Blessed are the
merciful:
they shall
have mercy
shown them.

Mercy comes
in many forms.
It is compassion,
or kindness
shown to
an offending person.
Though we often
think of it
in connection with
state or government
issues,
it's part of life
on a smaller scale
as well.

Mercy is shown
by parents
to children
repeating
the same mistakes
constantly
and on a
daily schedule.

Mercy is shown
by teachers
in the classroom
when they choose
not to humiliate
a student
in front of others
for a mistake.

Parents driven crazy
by a troublesome child
help both
themselves
and their child
when they temper
justice
with mercy.

The best
encouragement
people have
concerning mercy
is this:
if we give it,
we will get it.

HUMILITY

Humility
is not
breast beating
or belittling
ourselves
in front of others.

Humility
looks at all
the gifts
God has given
and recognizes
and cherishes them.

Humility is
the honest appraisal
of talent,
thanksgiving for it,
and use of
this talent
for the simple
joy of it.

When people are
gifted by someone,
they acknowledge
the gift
and thank the giver.

This is humility:
recognizing
our gifts,
using them,
and acknowledging
God as giver.

THOSE WHO MOURN

Blessed are they
who mourn;
they shall
be comforted.

Sorrow enters
everyone's life
at one time
or another.
We mourn
for losses
large and small,
each one
an ending
of something
or someone
very important
in our lives.

We mourn
our losses,
both tangible
and intangible,

with anger
usually beginning
the process.

We shake
our fist
at God
or man
and want to know
why bad things
happen to us,
forgetting that
death of everything
is as natural
as birth.
We are born
to die,
and therefore,
those for whom
we mourn
are ourselves.

KINDNESS

A gentle touch,
a thoughtful smile,
flowers appearing
for no reason,
compliments when
never expected,
holding hands
on springtime walks,
these are kindnesses
that free my spirit,
giving me a sample
of what perfect happiness
must feel like.

Knowing I'm loved
and cared for
makes me feel
so special,
it seems possible
to do anything I choose.
I give my love
to you in return,
not with conditions attached
but freely
and with abandon.

A gentle touch,
a thoughtful smile,
a little bit of kindness
are my gifts
right back to you.

JOY

Sometimes I'm
so overcome
with joy,
a whistle
or snippet of song
slips out of my mouth
unnoticed.

Happiness at home,
joy at work,
or seeing a new day
unfold before me,
is enough
to set my feet
tapping
and heart singing.

I celebrate
my family,
a roof
over my head,
a place to sleep,

schools for learning,
and all outdoors
on which to
feast my eyes.

I marvel
as scientists,
doctors,
and scholars,
discover
life's mysteries
and cures
in nature.

Many answers
can be found
by becoming one
with the earth.
And when we do,
we are filled
with joy;
not joy
tempered with practicality,
but pure,
unplanned,
overwhelming,
Joy!

WHO IS GOD?

God our Father;
God our Mother;
God Creator
and all knowing.

You have formed us
in the image
of your son
of humble birth.

We were taught
as little children
to fear your
perfect knowledge.

Gentle father,
loving mother,
through the years
ideas change.

You know every hair
upon our heads,
every need
and every dream.

Our vision
is so mortal,
we don't look
beyond this life.

We worry
about our jobs,
clothes for bodies,
food to live.

Yet you told us
not to worry,
that our needs
are known to you.

God our Father,
God our Mother
God Creator,
I believe.

BELIEF IN GOD

Can we look at
pores in the skin,
eyes that allow us
to see,
ears that hear,
a mouth that speaks
what the brain thinks,
a nose that smells
and breathes,
... and not believe?

Can we feel
and touch,
walk or sit,
or understand
the network
of our bodies
. . . and not believe?

Did all this,
animals, plants,
and minerals,
just evolve?
. . . from what?

There had to be
a Prime Mover.
It would seem easier
to believe in God
as the Prime Mover
than any other theory.

Indeed,
it would be
far more difficult
to prove these things
without a God,

however we envision
or name this Spirit,
as the Prime Force.

Jesus came
to tell us
there is a God
who loves us,
judges us wisely,
and nurtures us
as His children.
It's far easier
to believe this,
than to prove
otherwise.

I believe in God,
the Father Almighty,
Creator of heaven
and earth.
I believe it
because my existence
proves it.

OUR FATHER

Our Father,
who art in Heaven,
(and everywhere else,)
holy be your name
(used only in praise.)
Thy kingdom come,
(the afterlife
of each one of us,)
thy will be done
on earth as it is
in Heaven,
(there is a Heaven.)
Give us this day
our daily bread,
(we need only
ask and believe,)
and forgive us our sins
as we forgive those
who sin against us,
(must we also forget?)
And lead us not
into temptation,

(God never leads us
into temptation,
but walks
together with us
through it,)
but deliver us
from evil,
(as you said you would
whenever we ask.)
Amen.

OUR DAILY BREAD

All countries
have their own
daily bread,
each being
as unique
as the country
of its origin.

Wheat, rye,
bagel, donut,
French, Italian,
flat bread,
white, whole grain.
Each bread
can be a meal,
and often is,
when other foods
are scarce.

When we
have bread,
so often
it's taken for granted.
It seems

a daily necessity
we deserve
and therefore expect.

But that's
not always true.
Through no fault
of their own,
and possibly because of
the selfishness of others,
too many people
go to bed hungry
each night,
while others overeat,
overindulge, and overbuy.

God gave us
enough land and knowledge
to feed
the entire earth,
but we seem
to have trouble
with distribution.
We seem to be
hoarding food
. . . for what,
our trip to heaven?

FORGIVE US OUR TRESPASSES

How bold we are!
We have no shame,
it seems,
when sin is involved.
In fact,
to hear us tell it,
there's no such thing
as sin.
There's no punishment,
no Hell,
no Purgatory.

But just in case,
wouldn't it be wise
to hedge our bets?

What if there is a
Heaven,
Hell,
and Purgatory?
What if a God
who is completely just,
judges us fairly,
and thus decides
we have not
earned Heaven?
Where do we go?

What if God decides
to judge us
as we have
judged others?
We have heard
the parable
of the unjust servant
whose debt was forgiven
by his just master,
until he,
in turn,
refused to forgive
his servant's debt.
Then he was punished.

This is our example
given by Jesus
to teach us.

The wisest (and safest)
decision
would seem to be
to judge not
lest we be judged,
or better yet,
forgive as we
would like to be
forgiven.
We profit
by simplifying
our lives.

HOLY SPIRIT

Father, Son,
and Holy Spirit.
Elusive Holy Spirit;
how do we
explain you?

We understand
the role of
God the Father,
Creator
and Prime Mover.
We understand
the role of Son,
because God
became man
and walked the earth.

But you, Spirit,
your name is even
elusive.
You permeate our
conscious and unconscious
thoughts and actions,

challenging us
to become
all that we can be.

You are the
beginning of action
and the culmination of it,
infusing us with
courage and dedication
to bring out
the best
in ourselves and others.

You awaken
responsible adulthood,
putting aside
the simplicity
of childhood,
thus lighting the path
to wisdom.
Come Holy Spirit,
I am ready.

GUARDIAN ANGEL

Well, how about that?
You're back in vogue!
Although through time
you've been the bearer
of glad tidings,
commemorated with prayers,
and immortalized
in statues and medals,
you somehow were forgotten
by those you guard
for a long time.

You were out of style
as much as
St. Christopher
when we removed
his medals
from our cars.
It was as if
you were a fairy tale
some god-fearing people
chose to disregard.
"Protection" came from gangsters.

I'm delighted at the
turn of events.
Fate and religious fervor
are again in your corner.

Dear Guardian Angel,
always at my side,
I'm glad you're
back in fashion.
You've had to fight
an angel war,
then many
earthly ones.
Seems you're always
up for battle.

IMAGES

We look to images
to focus our attention
while triggering
prayerful thoughts.
We daydream
in any creative way
we choose,
remembering Bible stories,
then letting imagination roam.

>Looking at the manger,
>we think of shopkeepers
>so reluctant
>to become involved
>they turned away
>a woman in labor.
>The image of Joseph
>reminds us of this scene
>of a desperate father-to-be
>trying frantically
>to help his wife
>and soon-to-be born child.

The image of Mary

holding her new son,
starts thoughts
about the young mother
with questions
never alluded to.
What kind of mother
was this young girl?
Did she have
special talents?
Was she
a patient mother?

What kind of child
was Jesus?
Was he calm
or excitable,
friendly or shy,
talkative or quiet?

Images trigger thoughts,
helping us with
our friendship
and understanding
of real people
in generations past,
thus personalizing
our relationship with,
and adoration of,
God.

GOOD SAMARITAN

The bartender
had a busy
night,
with good tips
to take
on her vacation
next day.

Right before closing,
a local bag lady
came into
the bar crying.
She had been
raped, but refused
medical attention.

The bartender
summoned
her friend
the cab driver.
Taking all her tips,
she gave them
to the cabby
with these instructions.

"Take her to
a nice hotel,
give them
this money,
and tell them
to give her
a room,
a warm meal,
and anything else
she needs.
On my return
from vacation
I will stop
and settle
any difference."

A modern day
Good Samaritan.
I think
Christ loves
this bartender
a lot
because she
found Him
where He lives.

WORSHIP

Holy God,
Immortal Savior,
Loving Father,
Creator of the World,
how overwhelming
your titles are
to mortals on earth.

I praise you
as my God,
but talk to you
as my Father.

The world wearies me,
and I find
so little
understanding
and love
as I add on years
to my mortal life.
I long to talk to you
face to face
and feel

your comforting touch
on my shoulder.

Beloved son
of Mary and Joseph,
we hear of only one time
your worldly parents
didn't understand
your divinity.
When you were
lost in the Temple
they reacted like any
worried parents,
and then you
let us see
the face of God.

I'm also a parent
needing guidance
to raise your
precious children
trusted to my care.
Please help me
with this privilege.

TEMPLES OF WHAT?

People have been
referred to as
temples of the Holy Spirit,
a place wherein
God dwells.

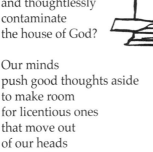

If this is so,
how can we
so willingly
and thoughtlessly
contaminate
the house of God?

Our minds
push good thoughts aside
to make room
for licentious ones
that move out
of our heads
to take shape
in actions.

Eyes view evil,
hands play out direction
from a sullied brain,
feet take us into places
where we waste our time.

We're a
health conscious
society,
always dieting
or eating natural foods,
jogging,
and seeing a doctor
once a year.

We worship the body,
but our souls
are left alone,
never cared for
like our bodies.
Yet they house
the Holy Spirit,
the Father and the Son.

LIVING IN PEACE

When we live
peacefully,
we're happy;
when we don't,
we're sad.

With this basic
knowledge in mind,
how can we live
other than peacefully?
Why do we quarrel
so easily at home,
at work,
or with friends?

Humanity,
with all its flaws
and shortcomings,
makes both peace
and war
happen simultaneously
in our homes,
neighborhoods,
and country.

The problem comes
when we try
to rationalize
why a country
is at war.
Why would anyone
war with neighbor
or family?

Could the cause
simply be
a case of jealousy?
Do we want
or envy others
lives or possessions?
Maybe *things*
have become
too important
out of all proportion.

We cannot
change the world,
but we can
change ourselves.
I leave you peace;
my peace I give
to you.

OCCASION OF SIN

As young students
we were told
to avoid
"occasions of sin."
In our innocence,
and with youthful
imaginations,
we conjured up
everyday happenings
as being potential
occasions of sin.

Being alone with,
or talking to
a member of
the opposite sex
might be one;
listening to
        bad companions;
        dancing too closely;
        overstaying a curfew.

As we grow
into adulthood,
occasions of sin
are looming still,
but now
we're supposed to have
the wisdom
to resist.

What are the real
occasions of sin
at our advanced
years and wisdom?
We should be wise
and have a
well-developed
sense of right,
but I'd venture to say,
rather a well-developed
sense of pride
has many feeling
they cannot sin,
and therefore,
there are no occasions.
How irrationally
we rationalize!

A MOMENT TO REFLECT

Too busy.
We're too busy
doing what
must be done
to relax
a moment
and reflect.

    A day in our youth,
    the first robin in spring,
    rain in summer,
    snow in winter,
    consistency in nature,
    are comfortable reflections.

    Aging brings more time
    for reflective thinking,
    but it's hard
    to find someone
    willing to listen
    to the reminiscing
    of the old.

What once was
regarded as wisdom,
a passing on
of hindsight,
seems now
a waste of time.

Too often
we're filled
with regret
because we didn't
take a moment
to listen to
another's thoughts
or histories.
Once they're gone,
questions will remain
unanswered forever:
a legacy
buried with the body.
If we're too busy
to reflect
on all our blessings,
history,
and nature's gifts . . .
we're too busy.

WORD OF GOD

Moses waited
to hear
the word of God
while people
impatiently
looked for
instant gratification,
forgetting miracles
so recently witnessed.

"I am the
Lord thy God,
thou shalt not
have strange gods
before me."
While receiving
these words
on the mountain,
Moses was unaware
of the golden calf
being cast,
then worshiped,
by the same people
so recently
led to safety.

"Thou shalt not
take the name
of the Lord in vain."
Doing so
is now so much
a part of
our daily vocabulary
we can hardly
express a thought
without God's name.

The Sabbath Day

becomes like any other,
we forget to
honor our parents,
sharp tongues
kill as surely
as sharp knives,
we cheer adultery
and bear false witness
while coveting
things belonging
to our neighbor.

We have heard
the Word of God
as carved in stone,
but do not listen.
How forgiving and patient
is our Father.

I LIVE

Oh God, my God,
let me get on
with my life.
I have lost;
I grieve;
will it never end?
My waking thoughts
are about
my lost one.
Days end with
the same remembering.
I am obsessed
with my memories;
will they never end
and let me
move on to today
and all my
tomorrows?

I have loved
and lost
but will
never forget.

Only let me
remember with joy
all the good times,
then help me
to not dwell
on the past.
My life is
also short.
I will reunite
soon enough
with my beloved;
this earth is not
my final journey.
I must learn
to live
each moment.

MORTALITY

Waking up this morning
I feel my mortality.
As my young son
once said
when he woke up ill,
"The colors of my body
are all mixed up."

It's hard to say
how I feel
except to note
the time
of my immortality
seems much closer.

My body is
no longer indestructible
and ready to
bounce out of bed
at a moment's notice
each morning.

Foods that used to
delight my stomach
can no longer
be accepted at all.
Arthritic joints
misshape my body
and the speed of youth
has slowed considerably.

I'm soon to be immortal,
but right now,
the colors of my body
are all mixed up.

DEATH

Death is rude.
It doesn't ask
our permission,
just barges right in
without an
"Excuse me" or
"I'm extremely sorry."

I hate you.

You put an end to
family
and friendships.
You don't ask
if we're ready.

It doesn't matter
how much we need
each other,
or if we've had time
to say our goodbyes
or prepare properly
to meet our creator.

You don't care
if we've had a chance
to grow old
and anticipate you,
or if we're so new
we can't even
lift our heads
to see you coming.

So I refuse
to give in to your
selfish thoughtlessness.
I choose
to rejoice instead
in the anticipation
of God's promise.

You have stolen
my life here,
but you'll never
catch my soul.

GOING HOME

How transient
is this life
we think
so permanent.

In our youth
we were certain
life on earth
went on forever,
but with age
came wisdom,
and often
aches, pains,

debilitating sickness,
and loss of memory
as well as hearing.

Our enthusiasm
for life
wavered,
encouraging
thoughts about
the next world
we'll pass into;
a world of
complete happiness,
lack of physical pain
and full vision
of our Creator.

How fortunate
our life of spirit
continues in an existence
we can't imagine
with mortal minds.
How sad for those
we leave behind,
but if we
believe the promise,
how exciting
to be going home.

EASTER

Hallelujah!
What a wonderful word!
It seems to be
a spring word
that pictures tulips,
hyacinths and daffodils
popping through
their cold soil graves
to give new meaning
each year to life
and the Resurrection.
Nature wakes,
as we must,
to listen to
the word of God
and believe.
Hallelujah!

ALL SAINTS' DAY

My dearly beloved,
I pray you have,
by now,
joined the fraternity
of sainthood
in the next world.

If so,
I'm curious
with whom you associate.
Have you met
the great saints,
Michael the Archangel,
or your own
guardian angel?

Is it old home week,
or is Heaven
sparsely populated?
What is God like?

What does
perfect happiness
feel like
when you see God
in all God's glory?

Does everyone
finally achieve it,
or are there
few in Heaven?
Do you ever
think of home,
or isn't that
an issue?

Compared to immortality,
is this mortal life
but a ripple
in the ocean
of eternity?

You lived;
you died;
you mattered.
I pray God
welcomed you
at Heaven's gate
with open arms.

ALL SOULS' DAY

(In honor of
Reverend Joseph Baglio,
based on his original
homily, *Life After Life*.)

We honor all
who have
preceded us
in death.

I began
in the womb,
and was known
by God.
The womb was
a comfortable place
where I had time
to form and grow.
Although dark
and airless,
it was comfortable
being with mom

all the time
and hearing her
talk and sing to me.
I didn't want
to leave;
it was so comfortable.

So God sent
his Son,
as a drop of blood
into my blood stream,
and his Son told me
I would be happy,
and not to be afraid.
I would be born
into sunlight,
and laughter,
and birds' songs,
and ski slopes;
so many things
I didn't know
or recognize.
But I told God
I was afraid.
I was safe
and comfortable
in my mother's womb.

And then it happened!
I exploded into
a new world,
and everything
God said
was true.

And then
God sent his Son
once more,
and told me again
not to be afraid.
I would soon
be born into
yet another world.
And it would be
better than
anything I yet knew.

It would be
better than the womb;
better than sunshine,
ski slopes,
birds singing,
family.

And then it happened,
. . . and I believe.

A PRIEST FOREVER

Memories of
Father Joseph Baglio
in his younger days,
pass softly
through my mind.
They cover over
forty-five years
of my life,
including early memories
of his twinkling eyes,
loving smile,
and bad puns.

He was every kid's
mentor, big brother,
and counselor,
sharing with all
who needed,
his heart
and shoulders
made big by love.

Teens were gifted with
Retreats, Masses,
Ice Cream Socials,
singing around the piano,
silly games,
and a devoted staff.

Father Baglio
started the Youth Center,
staying long enough
to work with
his first children's children.
During a time
of turmoil
in both Church
and religious life,
Father Baglio
was the steady oak
with roots
planted firmly
in the foundation
of his faith,
his love for God
and humanity
coming together
as one.

Father comforted
those who hurt
and those who mourned,
and when a burden
became too heavy
to be carried alone,
Father Joe was
there to share
the walk.

Father Joseph Baglio:
a priest forever,
and shining example
of birds' songs,
sunlight,
laughter,
ski slopes,
and family.

You are salt for the earth.
You are light for the world.

MATTHEW 5: 13-15

GREETING CARDS AVAILABLE
OF YOUR FAVORITE POEMS

MINIMUM ORDER: 12 CARDS

$1.50 per 5X7 Frameable card & envelope
PLUS $3.00 postage and handling

TITLES _____

_____

_____

_____

_____

YOUR NAME _____

ADDRESS _____

_____

_____

_____

PHONE (_____) _____

SEND TO: **ST. JOHN'S PUBLISHING**
6824 OAKLAWN AVENUE
EDINA, MINNESOTA 55435

FOR DISCOUNTS/MORE INFORMATION, CALL:
(612) 920-9044 OR
FAX (612) 920-7662

BOOKS AVAILABLE
BY DONNA LAGORIO MONTGOMERY FROM

• • •

Bread & Wine
is a spiritual look at each person's mortality and immortality.

Tea Party
shares short reflections about friendship, daily routines, and observations of life. Tuck in a purse and share with a friend at tea.

Coffee Talk
includes short reflections about women, men, friendship and families. Thoughts shared over a cup of coffee with a good friend.

Love, Life & Chocolate Chip Cookies
serves up a hearty helping of wit and wisdom in short quips on children, life and love in general.

Surviving Motherhood
A look at family relationships written by a mother of eight who is a survivor of motherhood herself.

Parenting a Business
looks at business relationships from a parenting standpoint.

Kids + Modeling = Money
is all you need to help your child begin a rewarding and prosperous modeling career. Discover the secrets of modeling success.

• • •

ST. JOHN'S PUBLISHING
6824 OAKLAWN AVENUE
EDINA, MINNESOTA 55435

Please send me _____ copy/copies of **Bread & Wine** (ISBN 0-938577-17-4). $14.95 each plus shipping.

Please send me _____ copy/copies of **Tea Party** (ISBN 0-938577-11-5). $14.95 each plus shipping.

Please send me _____ copy/copies of **Coffee Talk** (ISBN 0-938577-09-3). $14.95 each plus shipping.

Please send me_____copy/copies of **Love, Life & Chocolate Chip Cookies** (ISBN 0-938577-10-7). $6.95 each plus shipping.

Please send me_____copy/copies of **Surviving Motherhood** (ISBN 0-938577-00-X). $6.95 each plus shipping.

Please send me_____copy/copies of **Parenting a Business** (ISBN 0-938577-04-2). $14.95 each plus shipping.

Please send me_____copy/copies of **Kids + Modeling = Money** (ISBN 0-13-515172-4). $9.95 each plus shipping.

Shipping: $2.00 for first book. Add $1.00 for each additional book.

NAME_____

ADDRESS_____

_____

TELEPHONE_____